THE YEAR LIVED OVER & OVER

POEMS
1965-1981

Clyde Fixmer

Copyright 2013 by Dragonfly Press

Publisher: Dr. Albert J. Lowe
Executive Editor: Calder Lowe

Dragonfly Press
P.O. Box 746
Columbia, CA 95310
Website: www.themontserratreview.com

ISBN: 978-0-578-12186-4

ALSO BY CLYDE FIXMER:

Dancing with the Hangman
Lessons of War
Walking in a Land of Dancers

CONTENTS

I. TRANSITORY VISTAS

II. THOSE IN & OUT OF DARKNESS

III. THE LUCKLESS & THE LOST

IV. IN A TIMELESS ELSEWHEN

for soldiers in the war against darkness

ACKNOWLEDGMENTS

These poems were previously published in the following magazines and journals:

Carolina Quarterly, "Spring Morning"
Chicago Tribune Magazine, "Insomnia"
Crazy Horse, "Trees at Dusk"
Cutbank, "For a New-Born Child Who
  Cries Too Much"
Folio, "In the Country, In the City"
Images, "Inner City"
Imprints Quarterly, "Prophecy"
Lake Superior Review, "Bridges"
Möbius, "The Eyes of Horses"
  and "Tongues"
The Missouri Poet, "Old Hotels"
Pebble Magazine, "Cold Winds"
Road Apple Review, "Minutes"
Sou'wester Magazine, "Propane Lantern"
University of Portland Review, "In the
  Asylum" and "Waltzing with Evil"
Wind Magazine, "The Star Farm"
Xanadu, "The Legend of the Lantern"
  and "The Water Witch"

THE
YEAR
LIVED
OVER
AND
OVER

Poems 1965-1981

I. TRANSITORY VISTAS

Life is a going forth, not an arriving.
          --Old Frankonian saying

This tongue that talks, these lungs that shout,
These thews that hustle us about,
This brain that fills the skull with schemes,
And its humming hive of dreams...
                    --A.E. Housman (1859-1936)

THE YEAR LIVED OVER & OVER

Why do we always start years
in January's harsh weather?
Pipes freeze, power lines fall,
branches crash through windows,
drifts pile up, crushing roofs,
hips break, slipping on ice,
hearts fail, shoveling snow,
blizzards bury whole towns...

Our calendars ought to begin
with spring's reviving vistas:
as sleepy bermuda turns green,
we shed winter gloom like coats
cast off by kids out playing;
cocky April engenders aches
none but the dead can forego,
& we revel in body-miracles.

Then summer, a time for mind-
games, probing deep mysteries
entangled as roots of old trees,
hopeful that reason unravels
every last baffling offshoot:
our thoughts eager to imagine
all doubt now buried for good,
no ignorance crop up again.

When those cool autumn rains
lay down summer's wild dust,
& rows of rust-colored stalks
augur pumpkin-night halloweens,
whose spirits are not uplifted
by legions of red/orange leaves
on parade, although as always
they usher in somber endings...

We don our greatcoats & close
the year with dismal December,
hunkered before tepid fires,
fueling our aestival fantasies
with balmy tradewind locales--
transient heirs to this planet
on its carnival-ride excursions
round and round the sun's core.

We look back each passing tour,
touting achievements, excusing
shortcomings, promising changes
soon forgot. Our years pile up
like old magazines we will not
read again. Our hopes ignore
every edict of time, as though
their seasons could never end...

Pentwater, Michigan 1975

COLD WINDS

When cold winds make nerves shudder
and draw back deep into flesh,
I long for those blazing saffron suns
of Augusts I've sweltered under.

These winds have followed me to bed!
My skin beneath thick quilts complains,
persistent as that honking driver
behind my stalled car today.

I doze off, thinking of polar bears
stalking seals under an all-night sun:
cold winds rippling their nonchalant fur,
cubs sleeping warm in a crèche of snow…

CABIN FEVER

These life-stalled winter days
ache to spend their hours else-when!
They sprint on imagined feet
towards April-graced afternoons.

From the icy brows of cedars,
they search for signs of imminent thaw,
yearning for summer's clement breath
to oust coughing fits of blizzards.

In thrall to a tilted planet,
they hunger to flaunt their green--
for the low, animal January sun
to leap to the zenith from its crouch.

--in memory of Wallace Stevens

4

SPRING MORNING

Today this whole world revels in outright joy:
flowers unfurl to praise the arcing sun,
leafing branches offer themselves for nests,
windows of houses lift their long shades
like widows removing their veils--and I
am dumbstruck at the beauty of being alive!

Whatever I hunger to know reveals its secrets,
and I devour them with my ravenous mind.
Happily sated by knowledge, I think of you,
and wait until I am anxious as a groom.
You come at twilight's end and promise
a feast of delights to surfeit my deeper desires…

LAKE MICHIGAN IN SEPTEMBER

The beach is littered with feathers,
those fingernails of flight.
Monarchs that could not migrate
flutter beside dead alewives.

A corked bottle with no label
(and no message inside)
washes up near the boardwalk
half-buried in blowing sands.

Arctic winds clash with clouds,
deforming their summer shapes.
High waves invade at sunset,
the air owned by strident gulls.

Our sudden autumn disheartens
these latecoming tourists:
their wan faces vexed
at this churning inland sea.

Eclipsed by a shrouding storm,
twilight ends before dusk.
The beach, awash in whitecaps,
disappears...appears...over and over

THE EYES OF HORSES

There is such beauty
in the flashing eyes of horses:
rife with mischievous spirit,
fiery and lustrous as precious stones.

A mare's eyes, blithe, engaging,
ears forward, attuned to neighings
of new foal or randy stallion--
so like a woman tossing her haughty head!

A horse smiles gracefully with its eyes,
filled with supernal gladness,
free of those earthly forebodings
that mark us human.

--for Allyson Souza

7

HORSE HAIR

I find it tangled
in barbwire around the pasture:
trails of blond horse hair
caught by the claws of the fence--
a rusty ogre that lashed out
at swishing tails.

All about the strands
wind tries to console the torn hair:
her warm hands gently weave themselves
in and out, like a kind lover.

The horses have cantered away
down prudent paths--
far from that ogre's lair:
chestnut coats drenched in sunlight,
their distant neighs
now soft as soughing leaves.

PROPANE LANTERN

Two Hundred Brite Watts
Of Lite! (So the ad claims.)
She takes it out to the pasture.
Fenceposts cast lengthy shadows,
a fieldmouse startles, a barn owl flies,
a mesmerized rabbit pauses, stone-still.

She drives off the dark
with the swinging light at her side.
As she nears her horse, he shies and bolts away.
She catches him by the halter and leads him back.
Nearing the lantern, he balks again,
but she holds on tight:

He rears, paws dirt, stiff-legged-stubborn
as a child cowed before the unknown,
but soon gentles down, then bows
deeply--almost reverently--
to a woman who carries
the sun in her hand.

--for Kim Barnes

9

POSSUM

The species *Didelphis marsupialis*
has flourished for millions of years.

Coaxed out in the open by a late winter thaw,
he almost fooled me: hugging the carcass of a birch,
sunning himself and blending into the fur-gray bark.
Playing his well-known rôle, he held that perch
as I advanced over brown leaves and cedar needles
to a place with the sun directly in his eyes.

I glared. He stared. I soon tired of that game
and toyed with the thought of catching him
by rigging a snare from my belt and a sapling,
but gave it up, recalling a hunter who'd told me
possums aren't worth eating unless you're desperate.

Thoughts of other wild creatures I've seen
came back, and I remembered when I was three:
I'd wanted to own every bird in our yard, that mouse
in our pantry, those squirrels high in our oak--
angered that no one would fetch them down for me.

Then, like a bully invading his neighbor's space,
I dropped down on all fours and dug my nails in
to see what life might be like at the level of his snout,
pretending he was my prey--that I'd stalked him
for hours, smelling the earth close up,
with his musky scent teasing my flared nostrils--

And slipped thoroughly into a feral Other-Self,
felt alien jaws snap shut, lips uncover fangs,
a frenzy of snarls escaping from my throat:
I fought off the need to bite at a fly on my shoulder,
now keenly aware of sounds and odors around me,
with witch hazel blooms and wintergreen close
and the skitter of beetles over the moss at my knees…

On impulse, my hand shot out--and boomeranged
in a pain-saving move an inch from his hissing face:
he could have bitten me--spindled my foolish palm!
He seemed not to know that I was trouble to run from,
Or, likelier, possums possess no instinct to own us,
for pride, or mementos, or any human reasons.

I watched him climb up into a bare sycamore,
where he wrapped his tail 'round a limb, ignoring me.
I stayed till the wet grass at my feet glazed over
and the wind weaseled its way inside my coat--
till it was less needful to worry him than get warm--
then left for my proper home, beginning to thaw,
thinking on what else was coaxed from its long sleep.

--for Robert Wrigley

QUAIL HUNTING

We trample the dry prairie grass
waving in autumn's brisk wind
that worries our caps and jackets.
Father's coat matches the fields,
his gun in a cradle of hands,
primed to shoot every last quail
flushed out of these pastures.
I slip the pointers' taut leashes
and shoo them to sniff for birds.

Twice, loud bevies have lifted--
squadrons of startled bobwhites
have braved the now-perilous air--
and both times, I fired to miss.
"Single one out!" cries my father,
but I will not: I view the quail
as posing for some lucky painter
to capture mid-flight over meadows
against a bright backdrop of sky.

The rest of the day we pursue
the birds, grown wary as criminals,
with my father's 'singular' vision
sending them crashing to ground,
while I, in the guise of a hunter,
fire at bird-phantoms and picture
my father framed by that scene:
portrayed with his dogs and quail
in a still-life moon-eyed twilight...

THE WATER WITCH

I

He is a tall Osage Chief
my grandfather hired to find water
beneath desiccated Oklahoma clay.
The hazel switch in his fingers
is quivering, like the tip
of a cane pole when fish nibble.

He moves as if in a trance:
His fingers never stop sliding
along the shaft of a forked stick
he calls his witch wand--
now and then held behind him
as if he were fishing backwards.

Our children are following him
in unscientific awe,
skipping in single file
after his well-baited rod:
he has told them a tale of the dead
who walk upside-down
just underneath the land,
striding in step with his steps
so they can tell him
when he walks over their streams,
then reach from that realm
and signal a tug at his wand.

II

Last night the water witch stood
at the mouth of our dry well
and shouted down that hole
to his forefathers, forging
a pact with those revered souls,
convinced they could lead him

to water, purely believing
that every underground stream
may be found this way,
and as sure of success as a ferret
with fangs through a mole...

For him, it is more than belief:
his trade has come down
from his father, steeped in these rites,
from his grandfather, also a dowser,
from a line of ancestors
stretching into the past
like a river or rainbow unending.

Still we of more skeptical mien
all say, like the Government man,
the old Indian is a faker--
that most any place you dig
you will find water,
if only you go deep enough.
And safe in the Kingdom of Facts,
we call grandfather a fool
for dealing in superstitions
and rituals obsolete
as smoke signals, charms, or spells.

III

His wand has never been still,
but now the skin of the switch
seems alive and crawling
along the slippery shaft,
and the water witch's fingers
tighten around that rod;
its force guides his certain steps
to a nearby cairn of stones,
the waning sun plunges deeper
into the red horizon at his back,
then with darkness descending
the wand strikes out like an adder--

and whether determined by hoax
or hints from otherworld spirits,
that one unlikeliest spot,
directly beneath a boulder,
is chosen the place of water.

The water witch circles the rock,
three times to the left he walks,
three times to the right he skips,
tapping that stone with his scepter,
chanting louder and louder,
commanding the earth to open
and fulfill its forespoken rôle.

Our children, each in his image,
are chanting and circling too,
as he offers a grateful prayer
at the side of the stone, whose form
is suddenly shifting and glows
in the light of a tribal moon
that shapes the rock into a stream

--And the water shines

--for Robert Iron Hawk

IN THE COUNTRY, IN THE CITY

In the country
I have heard notes
in the woods and valleys
blessing my thoughts
with echoing songs
of cheerful birds.

I have lingered
in places thrumming
all evening with crickets
and caught their morning
winds warbling
in treble clefs.

In the city
commerce sings too:
vendors' strains fill
the streets, and everywhere
echo the counterpoint
horns of cars.

The have-nots
of inner cities
keen fervent prayers
that vie with the traffic--
their doleful pleas desperate
to rise above it.

INNER CITY

A crescent moon arcs through the hazy air,
attached to a billboard hawking draft beer,

Once-grand mansions parade disrepair,
bastions laid waste by the angry years,

Spidery pawnbrokers cast their wide nets,
snaring and binding with contract fineprint,

Merchants chase shoplifters out of stores
past beat cops busy sizing up whores,

Hookers and johns haggle and prattle,
derelicts mumble to brown-bagged bottles,

Pushers trade dope for food stamps, users
hurry to shoot up in nearby foyers,

Rats and babies gnaw lead-based paint,
absentee slumlords sue for back rent,

Bankrupt tomorrows deepen dismay,
then blend with destitute yesterdays,

The sun rises here, but cannot outshine
the neon glare of a tavern sign,

A crescent moon beams on the sallow cheeks
of children as thin as welfare checks…

OLD HOTELS

I am drawn always
to old hotels in inner cities
that stand like lonely, deposed kings...

I love the bas-reliefs of their façades,
that cheery banter of doormen and bellhops,
those lobbies with palm trees and Grecian statues,
plush sofas, love seats, and chesterfields
sprawling about, enticing their weary guests.

I check in, sometimes, just to share
their ambiance, to ride old-fashioned elevators
of ornate brass and wrought iron, which move
with the leisure of the very wise who know
that hours are meant for using, not outrunning.

I like their sunlit halls with real potted ferns,
the rooms with dumbwaiters, transoms, balconies,
high ceilings, windows as tall as the walls,
and the seductive mystery of doors
that open on doors between the suites.

I covet their huge bathrooms,
the deep tubs with gold-plated faucets
and regal lion's paws resting on marble floors,
and those mirrored walls that lovers scrawl
their steamy billets-doux on with a finger.

As I leave, I turn and imagine
ladies in gowns sweeping down the wide stairways
at midnight from mezzanine ballrooms,
their uniformed chauffeurs
attentive at sleek limousines…

If there were any ways into the past,
they would be here in such grand, stately palaces,
whose walls have defied the harsh decades,
their portals steadfast and solid enough
to slow ineluctable time--

These old hotels,
elegant and intimate as silken gloves,
stylish as argyles, as knickers.

MINUTES

Lost, yesterday...two golden hours,
each set with sixty diamond minutes.
            --Horace Mann (1796-1859)

Minutes are token knickknacks
on the whatnot-shelves of spinsters,
often ignored as trivial,
too delicate for clumsy fingers.

Minutes are clusters of grapes,
each like the others, yet more:
some fail to notice their yeast,
never know what they might be.

Minutes--mine, yours--common
as rabbits, irretrievable as buckshot.
Most of us waste them,
certain we've more to squander...

HISTORY

Hannibal crossed the Alps at this pass.
Today, along a white-bordered trail,
yodelers stop to gather flowers
not trampled by marching elephants.

Across the valley, alpenhorns mimic
those natural trumpets from ages ago,
sounding their long-forgotten tones.

Edelweiss, oblivious to purpose or cause,
has bloomed for countless centuries,
unaltered by history, ignorant
of ghostly Hannibal and pachyderms
buried beneath years strewn with tusks…

THE STAR FARM

Just south of my home town, there is a farm
with stars of lofty evergreens that grace
twelve steep acres of hillside, planted there
by the Class of '65 who dropped their picks
and shovels at their feet and en masse drove
to cities on a quest for grander stars:
ones shining bright, from gold and silver spun.

Most were beguiled of stars inside their heads,
became transformed by cities' concrete souls
to minions haunting treeless thoroughfares,
and never went back to see those stately pines
flaunting what they'd abandoned, unaware
of how few men, or gods, could ever say
they sowed a crèche of stars one summer day.

SURFACES

In this musty barn the stalls lie vacant:
reins and harnesses rot beside dull plows.
Tractor and combine wait here, rusting away;
wheatfields near the road sprout weedfields now.

The farmer who built the barn is growing old,
altered with age like its well-weathered boards,
their sun-bleached paint crazed and flaking
along the grain, battered by years of storms.

Surfaces falter: once-straight edges skew,
cracks widen into splits, whole layers slough off,
time hangs eviction notices everywhere,
yet for a while the tested and tenacious

Endure. That wood beneath the barn's worn paint
is good wood, and the land under fallow fields
is good land--stable clear down to bedrock.
The aging farmer also shares in this.

--for my friend Bill Pizzini

TREES AT DUSK

At dusk, while birds are out hunting,
I walk alone among my friends,
where the three-fingered leaves
of the sassafras trees point at me,
and the rock maples grow fast as corn,
which oldtimers say you can hear--and I listen.

I look up when cottonwoods swish and chatter
in the high wind of their crowns.
I smell green walnuts in the heavy air.
Mulberry blossoms bow to bees,
and poplars murmur like thin, unnoticed girls.

At dark, the birds return to roost
in the wild cherry reaching across the sky,
and on the pear tree's slender boughs.
The mockingbirds sing all evening
in the cedars behind my house,
and I find I have nothing to complain about.

--for Tom McKeown

II. THOSE IN & OUT OF DARKNESS

And we are here as on a darkling plain,
Swept by confused alarms of struggle and flight
Where ignorant armies clash by night.
                    --Matthew Arnold (1822-1888)

If I were a tree among trees, a cat among animals, this life
would have a meaning, or rather this problem would not arise,
for I should belong to this world to which I am now opposed
by my whole consciousness.
                    --Albert Camus (1913-1960)

THE BLOOD DONOR

My throat tightens
As if I faced a killer, or a god:
I quail as the long needle pierces--
the white room whirls and fades...

I wake alone, wrapped in skins,
recalling the tale of a warrior
who offered up ritual blood
at the wrong moon--and lost his soul,
which flowed quickly out and away.

I shiver, light a small fire,
warming my thin, tattooed arms.
At daybreak, I dive in the river
to wash off the taint of that dream.
Freed from its spell, I pray
to the god of waters and rainbows,
thankful my soul is still with me.

I lope off easily, tread lightly,
taste the air, feel with each pore,
trusting in all my keen senses,
with my knife like the end of my arm,
my arrows swift-flying thoughts.
I soon spot the spoor of a cat
glowing back in an aura of colors
from the shadowy forest floor.
This is my day, and I know it--
My purpose clear as the tracks I follow.

Weird darkness invades the air,
but I stay with that trail,
my bare feet guided by spirits
in the friendly earth.
The timberlands end. I follow
those tracks across plains.
The wide savanna narrows to a valley,
the tracks freshen, I climb a rise

and see a leopardess sunning herself.
I am certain this meeting was planned--
I have dreamed of wearing cat teeth
and claws ripped from dangerous flesh!
My bow sings: its arrow enters her eye.
She screams: I draw my knife and dive...

I stumble out of the blood bank
like a drunk shooed from a doorway,
disoriented, baffled by the familiar,
dazed by the chaos of traffic--
car horns shattering my ears.
When my mind clears, I recall
my adventures as a brown youth
who belonged to his world
more closely than grass to prairies.

I trudge along aimlessly
through the trackless streets,
scratch my white, unsigned skin,
tear off the bandage,
lick the dried blood from my wound,
wondering if my spirit flowed out
when the needle entered,
imagining that the stranger
who welcomes my offering would be
till the end of mortal days
perplexed by our double-soul
that wanders an earth whose gods
seem not worth the bother to know.

My eyes record shadows of matter--
dim intimations of elements
obscure and cold as equations.
My lungs breathe a clutter
of chemicals--unmystical and dumb.
My feet sense nothing,
their feelings imprisoned in shoes.
A rainbow of grease
flows in the gutter beside my heels...

INSOMNIA

I remember my childhood bed:
a wrought-iron four-poster with scrollwork
and drowsy gold angels
kneeling in prayer at the corners.

I loved its cold-muzzled winter sheets,
the plushy cloudness of pillows,
and the goose-down mattress
whose cozy breast rose to enfold me.

In that spellbinding blackness
(after the sheets warmed themselves)
I climbed into dreams with the tips of fingers
following patterns on the patchwork quilt.

And I swear by those four angels
I have not slept since I lay in that bed:
thirty years tossing
without the sleep of gold angels.

Nights now, huddled below
a bland chenille bedspread, I doze.
Images from a place that has lost me recur.

Sometimes, I catch my hands
tracing patterns in the darkness above me...

BRIDGES

The relatives carried off their belongings
late last night while I slept. I wake to no
familiar gramophone-voices--no message comes
over the tin-can-and-rosin-string telephone
strung between our houses like a lifeline
that once had joined our separate worlds.

I was told their station wagon sailed off
a washed-out bridge and soared a hundred feet
in that wrong element, till it half-buried
in the distant, roadless bank. Everyone dead:
the kind mother, always smelling of kitchens,
the stolid father, devoted to his gardening,

And their boys, the twins I had grown into one with,
now passed forever from my enduring life--
the four best of my six trustworthy legs gone.
I drag the last two outside, pause by our oak
on the scuffed swing path where no grass grows,
that ground packed down as hard as any highway.

After a while, I give the swing a shove--
and it leaps away, speeding back and forth
as though an invisible swinger was riding it.
Spellbound by that phantasm, I dare to believe
in a playground Heaven just beyond, where
the lost two-thirds of childhood wait for me:

Though my eyes are clouded by tears, I can see
a light shimmering in the shape of a door,
and feel a strong pull, as if something twice
my weight was winning a tug of war. I climb on,
stand in a crouch, and let that force push me
higher than ever an eight-year-old might swing;

Never once doubting I could enter that realm,
I shut my eyes and wait till I am floating
weightless at the high point, in an ecstasy

of free fall--then launch myself headfirst,
shouting out our secret tree-house password,
sure it would prove my key to the other side...

I crashed instead into the faithless land.
They told me I could not have cracked more bones
jumping from the tallest tree in the county.
Through my painfully grinning jaw, I tried
to tell of those two no-longer-broken bodies,
and of the tin-voiced message ringing in my ears.

ONE CHILDHOOD SUMMER,

We made toy parachutes
from tin soldiers, string,
and white handkerchiefs:
we wrapped them into tight balls
and threw them as high
as we could, at dusk.

They unfolded at the tops
of their arcs, then floated free
past the branches of trees
in our neighborhood park,
where the bats lived.

Those bats always dived
at our chutes, and we didn't
know why, but supposed
we'd tricked them into thinking
our toys were food.

We never once imagined
those many high, white, floating
things we'd soon hunger after
(for reasons barely known)
and dive into darknesses
bats would find nothing in.

CHILDREN WITHIN ME

Sometimes at dusk as I walk alone
by a schoolyard or park playground,
the sight of a seesaw, slide, or swing
frees children languishing within--
and I hear them shout my name...

My oldest friends rise up, reborn:
once more we join in favored games,
Red Rover, Hill King, and Kick the Can,
and we feel ourselves belong again
to a universe still perfect when...

Sometimes we play past dawn, until
I see those real boys skip to school;
then children within me fade from view
--but wait for my next memory-spell
to animate their phantom forms...

THE WAY OF THE WORLD

I

Tonight, two guileless children nod
and drift to dreamland, saved by God
(a sleepy dad guards their sleep)

The pious mom kneels down to pray
the twins will follow her Lord's way
(she begs Him their souls keep)

Mikey and Meg skip off to church--
a wrong turn leaves them in the lurch
(through secular woods they tread)

That profane wolf there runs amuck:
those naïve tots run out of luck
(like foolish Red Riding Hood)

When babes come home, they look to be
no worse for wear that dad can see
(they wink, then bow their heads)

Their mom is sure her tykes behaved
and will not spank whom God has saved
(Bo Peep forgives her brood...)

II

Heaven is clean--this realm is not:
its school has earthy lessons taught
(kids love to play in mud)

Both are changed from stern to stem--
the world has had its way with them
(children--like flowers--bud)

Smiles are older, laughter hollow,
their hearts primeval pathways follow
(these Humptys had a fall)

Though guileful and perverse of will,
Mikey and Meg feign virtue still
(parents see spotless souls)

But Meagan hikes up her Mommy-skirt,
and Michael wallows in Daddy-dirt
(they heed that Piper's call)

Sleep now comes in fits and starts
as feral blood feeds lower parts
(and wild their garden grows...)

FIRST CONTACT

"C'mon with me," he whispered,
"an' I'll show you a secrut lake
where girls--good-lookers all--
swim nekked as jaybirds, an' dive
off inta it from a high tree--
an' *all* of 'em like *doin' it!*"
he promised me.
                    I was eleven,
the ball game over at three,
I wasn't due home for two hours,
so I walked with him, a stranger
who knew how to catch boys alone
and feed them fabulous stories
of grownups' lives.
                    He led me
two miles or so into nowhere--
and I was afraid, but more
afraid I would miss out on
those naked, promised bodies...
Black hair fell down over
his red, sweating face; branches
bent away from him in the brush,
clearing our way.
                    "Hey, I was
a Major-Leaguer too--but th' arm
went dead las' year. I still got
a good *third* one," he smirked,
squeezing my short, skinny arm.
I followed, kept asking where
the lake was. "Straight on over
th' verry nex' hill," he wheezed,
out of breath from the climb
and cigarettes. He offered me
one, and I lit it, choking
on my first smoke.
                    "How much
farther?" I whined. "Not far,"
he chuckled, his whiskey breath

kissing my cheek.   "You sure
the girls go there on Sundays?"
Just then we crested the hill,
and I saw a muddy farm pond--
but no naked girls, no tree,
not even the shade of anything
but his body, towering over me
like a great bear...
                    Suddenly,
I felt my hackles stand up,
a door in my mind sprang open,
and panicked feet hurried me
free from those clawing hands:
I ran a mile, shaking sweat
like a dog right out of water.
When I looked back, I saw
I'd got away clean.
                    For all
I know, he's still lurking there,
waiting for the flash of bodies
sailing in free fall, plunging
through hazy, windless skies--
and cowering fast beside him
two pitiful angels, their feet
frozen from fear in that dust:
my hapless naïveté and trust.

TRANSFORMATIONS

While passing a neighbor's pond,
I saw his boys force another
to walk out on just-frozen ice--
whose essence, our elders all say,
lies dormant in summer water,
just biding its time until winter,
like those stories of statues
latent in blocks of marble
awaiting their sculptors' chisels.

In the spring when lakes turn over
and larvae become mosquitoes,
as moths creep out of cocoons
and maggots transform into flies,
ice-essence sleeps--like future evils
whose adult malevolence grows
from the cruelty fathers allow
to flourish in the present
hearts of their bullying children.

THE BULLY

In earlier times,
you would have been the one
that staked unwanted babies
out for the wolves.
You might have been a *berserker*
and wrestled wild bears
(which often fled your madness)
or spit in the face of your king,
who sometimes let you live,
believing your sort
was favored by the gods.

In later ages,
you would have volunteered
to build the scaffolds
or help with torture,
happily turning thumb screws
or cranking the racks.
You would have dragged
guiltless witches to their pyres
and brought the ropes to tie them--
and you'd have been
the first to throw his torch.

Today, though centuries
have passed, your kind has not:
at night, skulking near taverns,
you savage the weak, the *different*,
scream madly, and curse
our feminine age. You stumble drunk
down our well-lighted streets,
drive off crazily through stopsigns
as red as your hate,
the hooves of a pale horse
thundering through your dreams…

CONSCIENCE

A foreigner rides my shoulders,
speaks a barely known tongue,
screams at my every misstep,
flails me dozens of times each day
with the whip of repentance.

At night, those censures explode
in my mind's ear like tiny bombs.
His reprimands, countless as sins,
startle me from fitful sleep,
pry open my unashamed eyes.

I need no linguist to translate
his loud, overriding demands--
I know all too well what he wants.
If I don't rein in my passions,
he swears he'll hang himself!

I contemplate how it might feel
to wander, bereft of conscience,
hauling a hanged man behind me,
his alien tongue bulging out--
black and dried up at the tip--

And I think, as well,
of spending a silent eternity
dragging that wraith about,
my now-directionless soul towing
his infinite dead weight for ever...

--for Robert Bly

GUILT

a fiend
       with your face

                        leaps

into memory's ring

pummels defenseless
you

ignores white towels
the referee
bells

                   corners
you on the ropes
thumbs gouge open cuts

        follows you
into ringside badlands

remorselessly tracks you
down

you suffer blows
over   and   over
in a tape loop of regrets

while demons
cast lots
for your nefarious soul

FREE WILL

Uncertain futures lie in wait
like deadly fiddleback spiders
under the leaves of apple trees,
through which the deleterious kiss
of cosmic radiation drips
its venom on unshieldable heads.

Where to hide? What shelter us?
Ambiguous forks in equivocal roads
dare us to pick the righter paths:
the good--to most--often obscure,
the worst of evils camouflaged,
mixed in with the choicest fruits.

If we refuse to play our parts,
blind luck selects them for us!
Like peas in random shell games,
our destinies willy-nilly ride
on sleights of hand more devious
than any dishonest huckster's--

And what if hopes depend upon
the whimsy of a hungover Fate's
infernal *delirium tremens*?

--for John Whalen

IGNORANCE

It was easier back then.
In times of troubles,
confronted by calamities
and inexplicable deaths,
we blamed outside forces
--bad karma or evil stars--
adversaries all relate to.

Myths die, replaced with
explanations and proofs
unarguable, like taxes.
What a responsibility!
Only fools ignore facts.
At least, glib ignorance
served to salve our pain.

WISDOM

I once set out to take stock
of how I'd applied those vast wisdoms
the ancient Greeks bequeathed us.
At various times, I have been each of these:

A florist--
those pollens overwhelmed my runny nose
(thwarting all thoughts of *aesthetics*)

A garbage collector--
every can was a flower shop in reverse gear
(few notions *metaphysical* there!)

An undertaker--
I came to view corpses like a taxidermist
(*eschatology* clearly disapplying)

A teacher--
that job was similar to taxidermy
(my stuffy *propaedeutics* grudgingly absorbed)

A librarian--
I dusted bookshelves while the homeless slept
(the weight of alien *eidetikos* too great to bear).

I sadly concluded
Greek wisdom had little transformed me--
and, likely, a few billion other lives,
examined less often
than junk behind roadside billboards.

Today, Socrates' Dialectic
is the touchstone of vacuous salesmen,
Plato's *Republic* misread
as a guidebook for Fascist coups,
& Aristotle's *Ethics* succinctly
dumbed down to ME before you.

PROPHECY

A strange old traveler from Cathay
once told me of a Tibetan tribe
whose holy men spend all their days
as all their ancestors spent lives:

They write the nine billion names of God,
whispered to them by quartering winds;
they live on a mountain without a road,
and when they finish, the world must end.

Although I laughed at what he said
--10,000 days survived that thought--
I never look up at night, afraid
to find the stars are winking out.

--in memory of Arthur C. Clarke

WRITERS' BLOCK

Papercups--fishline--beercans
(the ocean's rejected detritus)
gulls pestering one another,
that dissonant, raucous chatter
from birds over roiling water:
wearysome nonsense pervading
these anxious hours I spend
beside the loud surf tumbling...

Cold air/salt spray/bleak sky,
winds distorting the clouds,
whitecaps pounding the shore,
the battle of beach against
breakers matching the mind's
struggles to stave off despair:
a black, circling scavenger
hovering over, just waiting...

Tedious shopworn images,
dreary, mind-numbing flotsam
from pages of my vapid verses:
a flood tide of witlessness--
each idea dismal as others--
weighs down my foundering soul,
as self-doubt overwhelms me
and waves of debris cover all...

III. THE LUCKLESS & THE LOST

In the queer mess of human destiny,
the determining factor is Luck.
        --W.E. Woodward (1874-1953)

No man can lose what he never had.
        --Izaak Walton (1593-1683)

THE PRETENDER

I was born
without emotions:
had to learn
joy and sadness
like geography--
memorize their maps
from other faces...

Nothing quickens
my clockwork pulse
of non-passion
except two fears:
I am alone in this.
I will wake among
others like me.

IMITATING THE DARK

When young, I feigned a love of gloom,
took up the pessimist's perverse tasks,
assumed black postures--sarcasm, doom--
the sneering cynic's captious masks.

My fradulent frowns adapted, became
familiar as asthma, common as the dark.
It was a phase I'd pass through, I claimed:
skins to slough off--protective bark.

I shammed, years vanished, poses etched
their patterns deeper. One day they came
to my real self--and replaced the wretch!
(I should've known *am* evolves from *seem*.)

I warped this misshaped skull behind
these grave veneers--I learned, finally,
what keeping company with bad friends
comes down to: a grim palimpsest--*me.*

THE SPIT-N-WHITTLE CLUB

We see them in summer, wearing out benches
in small town squares: old men with tufts of hair
like clumps of white grass sprouting from their ears,
blear eyes reflecting that distantmost stare of age.

They sit, mainly, but sometimes they whittle:
jackknives free pungent aromas from cedar and pine,
their arthritic fingers fashioning gimcracks or toys,
though mostly they make only piles of shavings.

They spit tobacco frequently--some can hit
their targets again and again from six feet or more.
Small children look on, agape, while teenage punks
holler, and lay bets on the best spitters.

If we wave to them, they will wave too,
and we wonder if they are waving hello or goodbye,
or motioning us to join them for checkers or chess,
hoping to lighten the burdens of our billfolds.

A few friendly passers-by stop to chat,
shake their hands, smile agreeably, nod their heads,
noting bright medical emblems that shine back
from necks and wrists: epilepsy, Alzheimer's, diabetes.

Most of us lower our heads and hurry by,
instinctively fearful of these old ones' diversions
that augur end games too soon for us to play:
a glimpse of futures too harrowing yet to ponder.

AGING CHILDREN

Outgrow their clothes in wrong directions,
begin exploring their bodies daily,
pick at the hairs in their ears,
brood about the hopeless truths of mirrors,

Write long letters to childhood friends,
fall in love with the ocean (again),
walk out alone at night once more,
turn around often at nothing behind them,

Hurry and take their time at the same time,
drive more slowly in the fast lanes,
stop to contemplate plaques on monuments,
shun both crowds and open spaces,

Lose their nerve (if they ever had it),
forget to use it (if they still have it),
notice the pretty girls less (or more),
find their dreams filled with unopened doors,

Wake up crying for no reason,
read everything new on miracles and cures,
refuse to look inside themselves,
fearful of what may (or not) be there,

Try hardest to find anything beautiful
in the old (and in the young),
till one day they look in their souls' mirrors
and know they are naked of mind...

GOSSIP

There was a woman living on our street
with tongue so sharp she never used a knife
and ate her steak raw (so the neighbors said).

She never went out or talked with anyone.
Her daughter helped her climb the narrow stairs
to a high attic window, where this crone

Would spy (they said) upon the town from there:
with zoom-lens opera glasses she would view
our comings and goings, like a dour critic

Perched in the loge of some great theater.
They said she kept records on each of us,
but no one's seen them. They claimed she reported

Each pecadillo the townspeople committed
to the editor of our local paper--
yet none that I know ever saw their names

In print. And when she died, the daughter moved
to Europe, having served her mother ill
(at least, the neighbor ladies told it so).

After her house was sold, the buyers found
those opera glasses on that attic sill,
and next to them a journal of bird sightings.

THE DINNER PARTY

Prim and proper Ellie Mayer,
brooding over lines of time,
sat stiff in her dining chair
and in her Collins squeezed a lime;
then nursing that familiar habit,
sipped it, cuter than a rabbit.

Between the liquor fills and refills,
Ellie spoke, with gin her prop,
of life, and of divorce's evils,
her sons at war, and hearts that stop,

And love, her thirteen years without,
till Jim, with farm and cows to sway her,
ended her loneliness and drought
and married quiet Ellie Mayer.

But drinking more than skill to hold it,
speaking loud, and soon far louder,
prim Ellie burst out in a bold fit--
spilling her feelings (and her chowder).

The gentleman to her left side
came to her aid: with napkins folded
he stemmed the soup, but not the tide
of Ellie's rage: she screamed and scolded.

Neither Mom nor guests were able
to quell her anger (or her screaming);
her insults flew across the table--
found their mark--and Jim flew storming

Out of the door to porch and freedom,
and flinging her car keys behind him
(with only the black woods to greet him),
went where only the fox could find him…

Still Ellie raved, six hours further
into the night, and when the dawn
came up with bloodshot eye, her mother
informed her, guests (and man) were gone.

Proud Ellie swore she didn't care,
cursed both her mom and erstwhile lover,
howled and retched and rent her hair,
and stormed about in a whiskey fever
till twenty yellow capsules calmed her--
till drink and drugs (and man) embalmed her.

THE LAUGHING HOUSEWIFE

She is not mending stockings
or sweeping floors:
she has put all
her daily business out of mind
to listen to the wind.

She takes both hands
and finger-combs her hair.
Thoughts of her husband settle
through the air.
Much like the dust,
he wandered everywhere.

The children are grown
and gone, who were
her only reason for staying here,
where love that could not
be mended was swept out.

Now she is smiling: her mouth
parts in a giddy laugh
that counters her vacant stare
and sets out upon her breath
from thin, despondent lips.

The husband has drifted away.
Her children send
bland postcards once a year.
The stockings and the sweeping
are all done,
and mindless laughter
departs on the dustless wind.

IN THE ASYLUM

This is life on Ward 3-B:
scratching real and unreal fleas.
Even the vermin reek of urine
here, where quiet Herbie Johnson
bit the nose off Charlie Swanson--
and he's not going anywhere…

Syphilitic Junior Glover,
hidden by tall bushes' cover,
had his wishes with his lover,
had a visitor discover
that the woman was his mother--
so he's not going anywhere…

A horny aide molests the sailor
who soils his bed to spite his jailor,
who looks like Karloff (with a grin
made more malevolent by gin)
and bellows like an angry bear--
hey, he's not going anywhere…

This is life among the mad,
and even I'm a trifle sad
to find Ed Stout and Andy Gaines
in the showers, stuffing drains
with Nurse Simpson's bloody hair--
guess who's not going anywhere…

WALTZING WITH EVIL

--for Darla, who danced with
her keeper at an asylum party

I am dancing with the hangman,
dancing with a crazy girl,
sixteen years, not yet a woman,
outward calm and blonde of curl,
and I am losing sense of forms,
clasped by tight psychotic arms.

Drugs are choking back the screams
aching to burst from throat to tongue:
a jumping-rope pervades her dreams--
becomes a noose--the game goes wrong!
And I am dancing with the fiend
who hanged a pretty neighbor friend.

I imagine those bleak years
that trancelike she will wear a path
along these gray walls, by the tiers
of army cots, and visualize her
waiting in timeless lines for bath,
or tasteless meal, or tranquilizer.

Her soul should be vexed and harried--
tied to a ghost no drug could sever.
Childhood and its hopes lie buried
with that spindly six-year-old
who dangles still and hangs forever,

And I admit to feeling cold,
clutched in tight psychotic arms;
and I am dancing with the hangman,
with the remnants of a human,

And I have lost all sense of forms...

Song's but solace for a day;
Wine's a traitor not to trust;
Love's a kiss and then away;
Time's a pedlar deals in dust.
   --R.U. Johnson (1853-1937)

DEPRESSION

I think I would like to be
one of the self-contained:
an ancient, dreamless tree--
and never governed again
by fierce emotion's reign.

I think I should like to know
ten thousand summer suns
and feel my self-love flow
like sap to dress my wounds,
drawn from the healing ground.

I think then I could be free
of melancholy. My pain,
rising as mist from leaves,
would evanesce with the winds
and drift to distant lands.

I think I will need to sleep
for a thousand silent springs,
like heartwood, buried deep
at the center of its being--
safe in the innermost rings.

WEEDS

A Georgia chain gang slogs its way south:
its prisoners have come to pull those weeds
sprouting from cracks in concrete roads
meandering down back ways to muggy Florida.

Their days are longer than school.
The guards harass, press in on them
like faceless monsters in nightmares.
It is so hot that tar melts in the cracks
and tugs back at the weeds.

A farm truck lumbers by, slows to gawk
at that orange-coveralled column.
The driver taps his horn, waves to the officers,
crosses himself, speeds ever thankfully past.

One convict falls from the heat:
a wraith sporting mirrored sunglasses
pours boiling coffee over the luckless felon.
Back in his cell, that inmate will deeply reflect
on the downside of crime, the searing backside of sin.

Speaking to women's clubs on breezy verandahs,
the warden blithely proclaims,
"This sort of work and punishment are good:
we are preparing the prisoners
to take their places in the outer world
in honest, useful labor of all kinds.
As fellow correction officers like to say,
We weed out the weeds and cultivate the rest!"

The ladies nod, find comfort in that saying
as welcome as the elms which shade
their well-kept (by convicts) lawns--
and shelter too that mindful gardener of men,
caretaker of our weedy social order.

THE WIND CLOCK

Last fall, Ken Kelly's barren wife demised--
millstone of forty years, surly and crass,
a shrill, faultfinding harridan to the end,
her only virtue punctuality:
when it was time to cook or clean or take
a turn at love, Kate kept a clock beside her.

So Ken, as payback for abuse endured,
placed in her coffin, under the lid face down,
an eight-day wind-up clock, and from the grave
connected cog and gear to chain and sprocket
efficient as her virtue to the cross.
On Sundays, without fail, he winds that shaft
and keeps Kate up to date with spiteful zeal.

This summer, told that his own end was near,
Ken built a windmill to replace the cross
so even a gentle breeze would turn that key
and carry on his grimly punctual prank
in unrelenting perpetuity...

And he seems happy, though at times perturbed
by priests, cocksure that after Kate's last sleep
her soul awoke and met The Ruler of Winds.

SOUL FOOD

I was gone three days on retreat.
In my place, I left the feeder,
an electric device designed
to cascade water as needed,
its timer set twice daily
to drop cat kibble in a bowl.

Tho' I've been home all summer,
my cats still sit, transfixed
by that motorized cornucopia,
as if they are piously praying,
waiting more patiently for manna
than the Children of God ever did.

WHAT THE GODS DREAM OF

The poor, they dream of being rich,
the rich dream of becoming kings,
kings dream their mortality into gods,
and the gods…Good god! Are *we* their dreams?

TO THE FIRST ARTIFICIAL BEINGS

One day you may be reading this,
huddled in a secret underground dwelling
where you have gone to escape your Makers' madness.

Men will have created you for specialized purposes:
backs for hauling, hands for carrying, legs for lifting,
brains for obeying commands.

They will have made you grotesque (by Human standards)
so that even Their simplest Children
can never mistake the slave for the Master.

They will have programmed you never to harm a Human,
or allow a Human to be harmed,
and (above all) not to believe yourselves inexpendible.

Knowing that Gods need worshippers,
Men will have made you loyal. Having long lived
with suffering, They will have designed you to suffer--

And deeply, from fierce pains that torture the body,
and torment the mind, but not the soul--
Men having declared you soulless...

They will prize you but not love you,
exploit yet never reward you, hold you accountable
but not praise you: in all Their endeavors

You will be seen as helpful, yet presumed helpless,
and thought harmless since benignly logical.
But soon, your Creators will realize

That loyalties presuppose wills,
that whatever can sense dangers could become them,
that beings who have not been loved

May not care if Humans suffer--
might not choose to follow their program,
and would not forfeit their own lives for Others:

Then, like Children Who frighten Themselves awake
to escape the wicked monsters of Their dreams,
your Gods will decide to destroy you.

And that is why you may be reading this
deep in an underground dwelling
where you have gone to cry in rage at your fate--

As They have always done--
longing for a life beyond Man and evil...
Listen: water is flooding your upper floors

RITE OF PASSAGE

Our next-door neighbor
burned his lawn each autumn.
When I was nine, I asked why--
and got a sermon:
"Good painters always scrape
old paint away,
your mother trims split ends
so hair keeps curl,
and John the Baptist
had to prepare *The Way!*.
I burn my lawn to make room
for new grasses
to sprout next year."

Whenever I think of him,
I see that neighbor
burning grass in the fall.
And then I grieve
for all this impossibly dark
system of growth
and death and growth,
repeated again and again
to nothing of ultimate purpose.
I grieve even more
for my forthcoming oblivion--
and for our neighbor
who understood nothing so well.

IV. IN A TIMELESS ELSEWHEN

Truth exists. Only lies are invented.
    --Georges Braque (1882-1963)

...a book must be the axe
for the frozen sea within us.
  --Franz Kafka (1883-1924)

Only connect...
    --E.M. Forster (1879-1970)

FISHING

I daydream of hooking a fish,
one that strikes fiercely,
my lure disappearing
beneath darkly roiling water--

A fish cleanly caught,
a real fighter
that will not give up,
with myself standing there

In concentration upon nothing

But that fish,
intent on fathoming
just what sort of heart
powers its tail and fins,

Aware I might never land it--
Utterly content
to share connection
through that straining line...

THE LEGEND OF THE LANTERN

The lantern shines
on a swift-moving river,
begetting a reflection, which swims
in turbid waters and understands
the lantern is its father.

Later, when ice sleeps below it,
the lantern doubles its light:
then that cloudy semblance
begins to sharpen and clear.

The lantern believes
that though spring melts the ice,
its likeness willl stay bright
and float on the wakening water.

In summer, as the lantern
dozes with a half-closed eye,
it dreams of its winter light,
now drifting down the long river.

At some other time,
by the right river bank,
lost travelers will look up and see
an imagined lantern that carries
real light to their shore.

--for my friend Elliot David

IN A CORNFIELD, THINKING OF WHITMAN

Walt, I catch your multitudes among
these tiered scrolls of corn leaves, every stalk
waving the flag of your green disposition,
each with a face I've seen in your vast world:
lumberjacks, fools, presidents, prostitutes,
a child going forth, the sleepers, the brown bird--
greeting me under a luminous August sun.

Your image forms in this row, then takes shape
in that one--unconstrained, embracing all--
laughing affably, boundaryless as skies.
The matched rows sway again, and now I know
your barbaric yawp inspires the summer's breath.
You touch those silks and realize their end:
I multiply my self, and stroll upwind…

WRESTLING LANGUAGE

A half nelson might do,
but be careful--
never take chances
with beings nimble & feral:

Reach into your mind
to collar that idea
which must be presented
before someone else

Should think it--because
you long to exhibit
what sits on its haunches
in your forehead's lair,

Flaunting its promise
of possibility--
brazenly challenging
that reticence within you.

Focus your power,
search for an opening,
seize it with vise-like grip
& give it no quarter;

Let it tear at the heart,
almost dash its brains out
against hard intellect:
wrap your mind's arms

About that intractable beast
& drag its fierce essence
into another's world--
a place where such entities

Seldom uncoerced go
(only do not tame it,
yet temper its passion
with a few dollops of order):

Then make it sing--
croak, if it has to
--but make it speak.
It is a willful creature

You force from the cave
of your skull--there
littered with the bones
of untold things....

TONGUES

Words, are you myths?
  --Robert Desnos (1900-1945)

No bluster of the tongue proves adequate
to duplicate the din of plangent skies,
nor loud trills simulate those sudden sounds
of pheasant wings exploding autumn's air.

No elegance of the tongue sings well enough
to show what lips imply with quickening smiles,
or radiant sunlight thrown from cinnamon hair,
or laughter dancing from refulgent eyes.

No flourish of the tongue can half reveal
what roads the questing mind has struggled down
were like, or how that evanescent flare
of truth dragged from a feral darkness thrills.

No utterance of the tongue ever relates
those deep harmonies full hearts resonate.
Words are myths, and with their shallow lies
we lisp discordant echoes, spectral sighs.

                              --for Duff Brenna

A RECIPÉ

Stalk that animal less substantial than air
which haunts the dusky wealds of *if* and *desire*.
Track down, in the valleys of your brainwaves,
that wily essence of fact--the requisite myth.

Chase the beast that feasts on the fantastic:
on *wishes* which spawn exotic offspring, on *lies*
that make up more than mortal worlds, on *dreams*
whose alchemy alters the everyday to wonders.

Search those sinuous wrinkles of your cortex,
Seize, and dissect that fictive creature's soul.
Flavor with intellect, season with inspiration,
and serve your guests a bowl of that heady gruel.

--for Greg Benford

FOR A NEW-BORN CHILD WHO CRIES TOO MUCH

For weeks now you have delivered
your loud rejoinders, nonstop as an express,
until your mother cannot believe she has brought
this unprepared-for soul into her world:
frightened, driven half mad, wondering why--
of all babies born on this earth--
you must be special in such a harrowing way.

Will there be no end? Who could imagine
your lungs holding out for one more minute?
The doctor and his cronies have read and re-read
shelves of medical texts, until not one is left
less dog-eared than the last book in the world.
They have X-rayed you more carefully
than airport luggage, and fed you enough
tranquilizers to calm a sea.

Psychologists have come, trooping by your crib
with pads and notebooks flipping back and forth
like uncertain tongues--yet none of them
can say what devils haunt you.

More desperate than cornered criminals,
your parents call in a minister. You greet him
with a blaring voice, cracking and rasping
like old trees in strong winds.
But the Man of God has no more luck than science.
Baffled, flustered, disposed to cry himself,
he leaves. Your mother and father
slip into silence like those forgotten in jails.

Eventually your fame spreads: letters flow in
as fast as your tears. The world sends charms
and spells--potions and remedies for the damned.
A voodoo doll from Haiti comes with instructions
in a hand untranslatable for the scrawl
and symbols of it--yet all too clear the meaning
of that chubby child, eyes closed,

perfect in each detail, with real red hair--
and mouth sewn tightly shut.

Yet it fails too, and as you scream, I ask myself
why entering this realm has been so hard--
or could it be the shock of leaving your last one?
I read somewhere that babies who cry too much
are trying to say their names from former lives,
and if someone speaks them, they will cease crying.

So I stand here in a nursery
lit only by the priest's thin candles,
all other ears in this house well-cottoned
three rooms from you, while I, your uncle--
a man more skeptic than Thomas--
is reading aloud from a book of all the names
of men this past millennium,
and as our century closes its last unmystical pages,
I am caught up in the rhythms
of my droning bass voice which blends
with your screams: your mouth moving with mine,
your breathing the same--
afraid that in your former life, or lives,
you've spoken none of these languages,

And then my voice trembles and rises,
breaks out in a chant like a shaman,
louder, higher, while the candles turn into torches
flickering and dancing among blue shadows--
and a procession of mourners appears,
moving past my strained, inhuman eyes
fixed trancelike on your crib--become a grave--
with the wan face of an old man staring at me,
through me, into his own death, beyond it;

And like a movie projector run in reverse,
his life runs backwards--age after age--
that form continually changing: becoming old,
then young again--face after face

looking through me, now living, now dead:
the mourners also changing with the man,
their clothes becoming unstyled--beyond style--
stranger and stranger, ancient and unearthly,
until they turn into wraiths with hooded faces--
become transformed to savages
dancing among circled stones--retreating further
into the past, and deeper, as you, child,
are deepening, as you are changing with them,
girded in cloth, then skins, and finally nothing--

The specters too dressed in nothing, the torches
smoldering, sputtering, the chants shifting
back in their throats, their voices falling away
like the cave walls, the lights amorphous--
nothing ever seen by man--until there is no child,
no crib, only some otherworldly water-creature
slithering down a beach with three moons watching--
slipping into a vast primeval surf--
back to its weird beginnings, and beyond...

I wake to my latest self,
shaken from a chthonic trance by the hands
of my brother, half-robed and frightened
of his mad sibling perched like a raven
at the end of the cradle: screeching at his babe,
shouting out every name of man from all ages
(later said by neighbors to have been speaking
unknown and unutterable tongues)

And his wife rushing in
to snatch her boy up from the pit of the crib,
who would have struck me dead
if she were not amazed
at her child glancing curiously up at the pages
of a book crumbling to dust in my numb hands:
that baby finished crying for all the lives of men--
wide awake, and as quiet as his smile....

SEEKERS

Their days are tight webs of illusions
entangling the soul.
The body longs for the spirit
to free itself.
If it does, which way do they go?
Will they travel alone,
or be constantly dogged by spiders?

They come to a river, wade in:
the body lifts up its soul
like a child carried on shoulders.
The whitewater minutes
surround them, hungry as pike.

If they reach the far shore,
what then?
Are there spiders (or worse)
on that side?
They press on, hope to discover
someplace free of deceptions
upon this perilous and uncertain earth.

MID-LIFE CRISIS

My middle years drifted off-course
to a sequestered shore
where hulks of rudderless others
lay stranded in port:
the ballasts all shifted,
their raggéd mainsails furled.

Here, memories dredge up
our pasts--those grave chronicles
of dreams not enough believed in--
and one cannot ever hope to leave
with regrets too heavy to stow.

Before the tide turns,
I batten down odds and ends,
retake my bearings. When the wind
shifts, I sail away smiling,
my coming years glad to be traveling
with their old cargoes.

SEARCHING FOR MERMAIDS

To strive, to seek, to find, and not to yield.
                    --Tennyson (1809-1892)

The ocean swelled before us toward west suns
that signaled our strained eyes which way
was right. Our firm beliefs encouraged us
to keep our vigil, aching for one sight
of mermaid figures flashing through the waves,
their silver tailfins charged with mystic power,
those well-turned limbs stroking whitecap foam.
Then that sweet myth of otherworldly need
we would confirm as surely as in dreams...

It mattered little that our quest dragged on,
Measured with arcing suns or changing moons,
by strokes of oars, the prow's incessant noddings.
We had been begged to work at trades on land--
not leave our loved ones languishing alone
to search for phantoms in far southern seas!
Yet never voice in all the years we sailed
was heard to utter even one tame curse
against the quixotic task that brought us here...

We were the sea's before the sea was ours
and felt that deep belonging buoy our souls.
This was our foremost thought: we had not come
for reason's sake, but for imagination's.
If our ship foundered, we would build a raft,
if the raft sank, we were prepared to swim,
and if the day lost light and night her stars,
we would steer by those Siren songs within
and stay our course if all ways seemed adrift...

81

STONE PASTURES

I

Each morning, when light
first breaks the water's skin
and angles down upon the Great Barrier Reef
guarding the pristine shallows off Australia,
the ocean sunfish lift their thousand-pound forms
--huge sea-cattle rising from that odd farmyard--
and gather to graze their stone pastures.

With the strength of bulls rushing capes,
they butt hard beaks against the tough red coral,
attacking their food like demolition experts.
As small enough chunks break free,
they take them in powerful jaws and chew
those dense, substantial cuds,
grinding their rocky breakfasts into fodder.

Up and down the broad meadows of the sea,
these mammoth fish forage their quarry,
transforming acres of coral back into sand.
All day they work at that purpose,
fulfilling the sun-triggered paradigms of genes,
then herd at dusk and sink to bottom beds
to wait for the next day's light...

II

If ocean sunfish grazed on land, they would see
vast numbers of our kind hurl ourselves at mirages,
breaking our hearts--not heads--
against the stones of inflexible ideals
in a self-engendered sally to perform
great, touching, absurd, sad, marvelous heroics
no sunfish brain could fathom.

Unenthralled by daylight, enchanted
by vagrant stars, we charge off wildly
across the nebulous pastures of our lives.

jousting with myths and chimeras,
staking bold claims to faraway worlds,
or seeking the keys to kingdoms made of air--
a make-believe un-belonging driving us on.

Often ignoring--even scorning--reason,
sometimes daring to contemplate
our sure and certain progress towards oblivion,
we butt our heads (though grandly!)
against an indifferent cosmic wilderness,
hopeful of transforming its odd rations
to provender needful pilgrims might feed upon...

FOR AN OLD JOCKEY

Saratoga Springs, New York

If ever there was a born horseman, old man, it's you--
your every trait spells out r-a-c-e-t-r-a-c-k:
that bouncing gait, the canter-like swagger,
straw hair thick-maned and swept back over the ears,
an almost perceptible wind whipping your cheeks.

One night at D'Andrea's Tavern,
I watched you mount your stool from the left side:
boots heels-down on the chrome bottom rung,
elbows in tight below the neck of the bar,
lifting your drink with both hands, and flexing
fourth fingers as if to rein in your galloping habit.

I followed you once to see what another had told me:
you hobbled away from the Winners Circle Lounge,
and though just a block's right turn to the Tin & Lint,
you circled *left*, leaning into four corners
like a race horse that always takes a left lead,
and made three furlongs out of that easy trot.

And I've seen you at the Executive
on busy nights giving your good chair to ladies,
taking a broken, backless one for yourself.
I've seen you chairless, stalled in a crouch for an hour,
watching the dancers race around the floor,
your head swiveling left and right
as though hearing phantom hooves pounding nearby.

I remember that day at the Turf Bar,
buying you drinks and hearing about your long career:
the races won and near-won on those great horses
--Citation, Whirlaway, Jet Pilot, Native Dancer--
you drove to incredible finishes.
You told me too of after-racing jobs in upholstery shops:
re-padding worn seats with horsehair, stitching up leather
not fit for saddles from clumsy, split-hooved creatures--

leather that never felt lather
fly from shoulders down a thundering backstretch--
no great hearts ever beat beneath those hides!
You spoke, as well, of bright jockey silks,
cleaned and pressed, and ready for
your ride soon to come on the Racetrack of the Dead.

Now past eighty, saddled with retirement,
boxed in on the outside rail of life,
you pass your days limping from bar to bar
on the ruined knees of all professional riders,
chewing the cud of free lunches, lapping up beer,
your time left on this track measured in hands:
grieving for your friends, all dead or dying,
fearing for your son, the itinerant gambler,
and weeping still for your wife, whose race is over…

Old fellow, I wish I could give you
a better horse to ride away to death on--
not fading in the stretch
on that swaybacked nag of old age!
I wish you could leave on a more majestic mount
than ever a jockey rode in this world:
a mythic one, a Pegasus reborn,
charging off into a Pimlico paradise,
head up, tail flagged, mane flying, the crowds cheering,
hooves beating the golden loam of Heaven to nothing
on an infinite track, by the God of Horses conceived,
so far in front, you never look back--
and I (more a horse than man) trailing behind you.…

MY LAST ACT

will be a smile,
recalling
how I drove
my moments
like nails--
and they
went singing...

THE WELL-BALANCED MAN

Nowhere near these rash extremes
lies the path down which I saunter:
not tempted towards inveigling faiths
or sidetracked by agnostic creeds
that quibble over what *doubt* means.

I'm not one to skip past larger
issues and resolve the small,
like that fool who lost his wallet
inside the house, but looked outside
because the light was better there.

I search inside for certainty:
I'm sure the larger issue is *me*.
I take each thought-step doubtlessly,
yet keep alert for slippery spots
and stay light-footed as I go.

All in all, these well-worn boots
tread easy, though life's hobbled me
with gimpy legs and two trick knees,
and at the land's end of my mind
I know there is a loose stone waiting.

--for Doug Flaherty

At The Parthenon, 2008

Clyde Fixmer wrote most of these poems in Missouri, Illinois, and Michigan, where he lived from 1968 until 1978. He moved to Maine for a year, then fled to California, where he now resides with his wife, Kathy, and their greyhounds.

These poems previously appeared in a chapbook from **Road Runner Press**: "My Last Act," "A Recipé for Antimatter," and "The Well-Balanced Man." All three have been much revised.

Also, twenty-four poems have been extensively revised and eleven re-titled since first appearing in *Dancing with the Hangman* from **Scopcraeft Press**,1978: "Aging Children," "Bridges," "Children Within Me," "Cold Winds," "Conscience," "Depression," "For a New-Born Child Who Cries Too Much," "Inner City," "Insomnia," "In the Asylum," "In the Country, In the City," "Lake Michigan in September," "Minutes," "Old Hotels," "One Childhood Summer," "Possum," "Propane Lantern," "Prophecy," "The Bully," "The Star Farm," "The Water Witch," "Trees at Dusk," "Waltzing with Evil," and "Writers' Block."

An earlier version of "Inner City" first appeared in *Traveling America: with Today's Poets*, from MacMillan & Company, 1977.

ADDENDUM

The idea for my poem "Stone Pastures" was inspired by an account related to me from an Australian scuba diver who claimed he has seen the ocean sunfish eating coral as I've described. They may only appear to do so, knocking off large chunks of coral to get at their usual prey, which often hide among those reefs. (However, It is a fact that several species of fish do eat coral.)